gone country

gone country

portraits of country music's new stars

raeanne rubenstein

introduction by chet flippo

SCHIRMER BOOKS
AN IMPRINT OF SIMON & SCHUSTER MACMILLAN
NEW YORK

PRENTICE HALL INTERNATIONAL
LONDON • MEXICO CITY • NEW DELHI • SINGAPORE • SYDNEY • TORONTO

Schirmer Books
An Imprint of Simon & Schuster Macmillan
1633 Broadway
New York, NY 10019

Library of Congress Catalog Card Number: 96-6613
Printed in the United States of America
Printing Number
  2 3 4 5 6 7 8 9 10

Design by Elizabeth Van Itallie

Library of Congress Cataloging in Publication Data
Rubenstein, Raeanne.
Gone country: portraits of country music's new stars/Raeanne Rubenstein; introduction by Chet Flippo.
p. cm.
ISBN 0-02-864594-4
1. Country musicians—United States—Portraits. I. Title.
ML87.R79 1997
781.642'092'273—dc21   96-6613
[B]   CIP
                                                  MN

This paper meets the requirements of ANSI/NISO Z39.48-1992 (Permanence of Paper).

this book is dedicated to my parents,
sylvia and isidore rubenstein

contents

credits

A very heartfelt thank you to the following friends who contributed their unique talents, creative vision, and their time to this project.

DROPS EVERYTHING: Nashville's premiere custom and rental backdrop company catering to the photo, video, and concert tour industries. All the painted backdrops in this book were created by them. Phone: (615) 333-0401.

HOLLY BALLARD: Easygoing and creative, Holly Ballard did the hair and makeup in no time at all for the very hip Mavericks. She works on a wide variety of projects with many different artists, and can also be found at her salon, in the heart of Nashville's music community. Phone: (615) 321-0390.

MARY BETH FELTS: Freelance makeup artist Mary Beth Felts was frequently requested by the artists in the book. Her spectacular makeups include Martina McBride, Suzy Bogguss, James House, and Shelby Lynn. Phone: (615) 662-6617.

LINDA DeMITH: Six-time Emmy Award–winning hair and makeup artist Linda DeMith has worked with many recording and film stars for 20 years. She can be found at her upscale salon and showroom across from the new arena in the heart of downtown Nashville. For this book, she worked her magic on Tanya Tucker. Phone: (615) 726-2222.

NAMASTE ACRES BED & BREAKFAST: Nestled deep in the hills of Williamson County, Namaste is a fun place. The comfortable inn boasts large western-influenced guest rooms, a barn for your horses, a pool, peace and quiet, and some of the best antique shopping available in nearby Leipers Fork and Franklin. The eventful photo shoot of Doug Supernaw took place there. Phone: (615) 791-0333.

RIQUE: Popular image stylist Rique is also proprietor of one of Nashville's premier salons, where many a famous face can be seen. Currently dividing his time between Nashville and Los Angeles, Rique can be found on many a photo, video, or movie set. Although you cannot see it in this book, the hair he created for Emmylou Harris is painted blue. Phone: (615) 292-9041.

RONDALE OVERSTREET: Talented hairstylist Rondale creates uniquely original styles for each of her celebrity clients. Splitting her time between Nashville and her home base of Fairhope, Alabama, she can be found both in the salon and on the set. She did the fabulous hair for the many Shelby Lynn pages in this book. Phone: (334) 928-9201, ext. 6744.

In addition, I would also like to thank the friends and colleagues who went out of their way to lend their support to this project. May you live long and prosper!

First and foremost is **BONNIE GARNER,** talented manager of Marty Stuart, who put me up and put up with me for the yearlong duration of this book. Also at the top of the list is **EVELYN SHRIVER,** who encouraged me to do this project in the first place, and then never failed to give her support and honest opinion at every opportunity. **GERRY WOOD,** busy reporter, talented writer, friend, and, most of all, sidekick on some pretty extraordinary adventures—some humorous, some not—this book could not have happened without him. **CHET FLIPPO,** talented writer and longtime friend, who "got" the pictures right away, and was able to express them in words. **BRYDGET CARILLO,** my talented assistant, friend, and ceaseless morale booster, throughout a really wide variety of photo situations. Also, **MARK BOUGHTON,** patient and supportive, humorous and helpful, at all times. Fortunately for me, I met **ANGIE CARROLL,** my Middle Tennessee State University summer intern, whose versatility, sensitivity, and talent never ceased to amaze me. **SHARON ALLEN** and **ANGELA VAN VRANKEN,** who believed in this project from Day One, and put themselves on the line to help me. **CATHY GURLEY,** who put the tremendous weight of her experience and prestige behind me, and helped me out of friendship. **BILL IVEY** and **DIANA JOHNSON,** at the Country Music Hall of Fame, who made me aware of the long-term significance of this project in the first place, and **PAUL KINGSBURY** and **DAN COOPER,** who wrote such inspiring words about the work. In addition, I wish to thank **DIANA HENDERSON, TK KIMBRELL, MERLE KILGORE, JAN SNYDER, SUSAN SIZEMORE, BILL LOKEY, SANDY NEESE, JEANNIE MILEWSKI, HOLLY GEORGE WARREN, SHERBE GREEN, DEBBY HOLLY** and **SUMMER HARMON, MARTY STUART, ROGER SOVINE, MIKE JONES, ERIN MORRIS** and **JIM DELLACROCE, ROBERT REYNOLDS, RONNA RUBIN, JERRY STROBL, MARSHALL CHAPMAN, MELISSA MATTHEWS, PATTI BOWMAN, JEANNIE POLLOCK, BELLA STRINGER, MEREDITH IRWIN, SHELBY LYNN, PHILLIP TUCK, DAVE PEDERSON, DAVE MEREDITH,** and the folks at **CHROMATICS** and **DURY's,** whom I saw every day. I also especially wish to thank my editor at Schirmer Books/ Simon & Schuster Macmillan, **RICHARD CARLIN,** for helping with this project in any way possible and for always being there for me, the publisher, **PAUL BOGER,** for all his support, and finally to **ALICIA WILLIAMSON,** always the cheerful and helpful one. Long May You Reign!

preface

Recently, "TNN Country News" broadcast a feature about me and the work I was doing to create this book. On various occasions, they came to a photo shoot and filmed it; later, they interviewed me. As it happened, I was with some friends at a Mexican restaurant in Nashville when the segment aired. My friends cozied up to the bar to watch it on the TV, while I stayed at the table, vaguely embarrassed. I couldn't hear a word, but I could see it very clearly.

What I saw was lots of busy people, my friends and colleagues, doing their thing: applying makeup, arranging lights, discussing layouts, ironing wardrobe. At various moments I saw lots of famous faces, sometimes in curlers in a makeup room, or in a pool, or a hay field, always surrounded by the apparent mayhem.

In the midst of it all I saw myself, dressed in black, in sneakers, without makeup, sometimes wearing a baseball cap, upstaged by the scene. I looked absorbed, oblivious to the camera crew, distant. In fact, I was seeing myself at work but I didn't look at all the way I imagined I would.

The scenario looked cool; the stars looked great, my staff looked hip. Why did I look so out of it? I wondered. As I watched us on the TV screen, I tried to remember what I was thinking about when I was actually in the situations I was now watching. And then I knew what it was: I was thinking about what I call the "Big Idea."

The "Big Idea" is what makes a photograph a great photograph. It is the tantalizing quality that makes an image once seen, never forgotten. It is the intelligence that illuminates all great works of art in any field. It is what drives artists mad because it does not appear on command.

In some cases the "Big Idea" comes in advance; you think of it in time to prepare, get props, clothes, wigs, or whatever to make it happen. Then it is a simple matter to realize; you just put it together the way you imagined it. This, by the way, is a very heady experience.

Sometimes, the "Big Idea" is served by serendipity. You cannot think of it until the moment of the photo shoot (some people might call this being "unprepared") when the artists themselves or a guardian angel say or do something that allows the perfect way to portray that person to pop into your mind. This works as long as the idea comes in time, i.e., before the shoot or at least during it. It is a cause for despair if you think of it when the artist is already gone.

Sometimes the "Big Idea" never comes.

Which is why I looked so distant on the TV screen. I was absorbed with the hope of creating a great photograph.

I decided there and then never again to be filmed while actually shooting; I just look too damn uncool!

A couple of days later, a letter arrived. It was hand addressed and came from Alabama. This is what it said:

Raeanne,

Hey. My name is Courtney Pene. I am almost 15 years old. I wrote you for a few reasons. I saw the "TNN Country News" w/you on it, anyways I wanted to talk to a photographer because I want to be one when I get older, for a country magazine. So can I ask you about being a photographer? Well first, how did you get started? Is it a hard job? Do you get to travel to places? Do you work for any magazines or for yourself?

See, I love taking pictures. At concerts, I run out of film so fast, and I just take pictures a lot.

Can you give me any advice?

Well please write back!

P.S. I *loved* all your pictures. Esp. the Bryan White one! You have great ideas!!

Courtney Pene

Much to my amazement, someone had gotten the point! It got through to Courtney Pene and, I hoped, to others. I felt a lot better.

By the way, when I was Courtney's age, I was exactly like her. I loved taking pictures. At concerts, I would always run out of film too fast. But I came up with a solution that she hasn't thought of yet. You shoot the same rolls of film again! The technique works best if you change your lens to one with a much longer or much shorter focal length than the one you used the first time around. This technique works great in live concert situations because the pictures look so exciting, plus you don't need much film (the main thing). Anyway, I established my career doing this; in fact, I became famous for it.

Shortly after the double-exposure phase of my career ended, I got one of my first assignments: go with a reporter to Nashville and photograph some of the country singers there (Wow! Business travel!). So I got on a plane and went to Music Row, which I remember as blocks of small, stone, four-square style houses, connected by dirt roads (I may have that part confused), each with the name of a country singer on the door. We interviewed Mel Tillis, Sonny James, and others at that time.

Next, we went to the "Johnny Cash Show" (I think it might have been taping at the Ryman but I'm not sure). The reporter and I went in the building and no one stopped us. We were supposed to have an appointment to interview Johnny Cash, but no one seemed to know anything about it. Mr. Cash was just several feet away, but he always seemed to be in the middle of something, and anyway we were afraid to speak to him (dangerous man, always wore black, we had been told). After what seemed like hours, I gave up and sat down at the edge of the stage. Then (I swear this is true) a huge shadow passed over me and I looked up. It was Johnny Cash himself, and he said, "Hello, little lady, can I help you with something?"

When I photographed him this year, I told him that story. He laughed out loud and said, "I like you because you're polite!" But, in the end, he didn't remember the incident.

We also visited Leonard Cohen on his Nashville farm on that trip (I had never been to a farm before; most people don't know that Leonard Cohen ever lived in Nashville). Last year, my picture of Leonard Cohen taken on that trip was published in *Rolling Stone Images of Rock & Roll*, the magazine's homage to great music photography. I was honored, and inspired to think about the qualities of great photographs that stand the test of time.

Several years later, Peter McCabe became the editor of *Country Music Magazine*, which was a feisty start-up at the time. He gave me an assignment that changed my life: photograph Waylon Jennings, the country music outlaw, who was appearing in New York City at the then-infamous club, Max's Kansas City. All I can say is, Waylon (and his band) were not from the "polite" side of the country music street. I thought they were a blast.

One thing led to the next, and before I knew what had happened I found myself living in Nashville, working on my first photo book of country stars and their life-styles, tour buses, charity sports events, country kitsch homes and cars, and exotic and glittery costumes. That book was called *Honkytonk Heroes*, in deference to Waylon and Willie.

This reminds me of the main point: why I did this book! I believe that the pictures I take are infinitely more significant than I am, that they are moments in time never to exist again. In a strangely beautiful way, their importance exceeds even the artists who appear in them. A photo I did in 1975 of Roger Miller, sitting at the edge of Old Hickory Lake with the sun sinking behind him, holding a lit cigarette lighter in front of him in a very formal, ritualistic way, is an example. At the time, the photo was interesting. Now it's mythology!

I really enjoyed living in Nashville at that time, and I wanted to stay. But I went back to New York anyway.

Twenty years have passed since these events transpired, although it seems like yesterday to me. After all these years, I saw Bill Anderson one day backstage at the Grand Ole Opry and he said to me, "Raeanne, where have you been? I haven't seen you for a while."

In those twenty years, some things have changed (definitely no dirt roads on Music Row now) but it is truly remarkable how much has stayed the same, true to its roots, as they are fond of saying in Nashville. There are a few larger buildings on Music Row, although the four-squares are still there. Dolly Parton still reigns as the undisputed Queen of Country Music, although Reba, or Trisha, or Patty may be the next. Garth may sell zillions of records, but the Highwaymen still tour (raucous and unruly as ever I remember, I might add), and the people are still friendly, the countryside is still beautiful, and the chiggers still bite.

The business is bigger. There are more managers, more publicists, more artists, more money! But busy artists still contribute an amazing amount of their time and resources to a variety of charitable causes. And the glittery Nudie suits of yore are more popular than ever among the younger artists who surely think that Manuel is country couture.

But I'm not really interested in that. It's the photos themselves that matter to me—their timelessness, their beauty, their truth. It's the challenge of making images of country artists that will still mean something in the future, that will make us smile and say, "I remember them," or "I remember that" in a direct way, as though we had been there ourselves, even if, like Courtney Pene is now, they are "almost" 15 years old, sometime in the future.

I truly enjoyed working with every artist who contributed their time and their visages to this book. They have proved to be imaginative, fun-loving and cooperative to the max, often coming up with the ideas for the pictures themselves (I'll never tell you which ones; I want *all* the credit!). As Neal McCoy said to his publicist when she objected to one of my ideas, "Let her do what she wants. It's her book!" Thanks for that, Neal, and all of you!

If, by the way, your favorite artist is not in this book, I'm really sorry! There are so many more artists recording and performing today than ever before that we just ran out of pages. We attempted to use our crystal ball, and guess, based on an artist's track record, commitment to their craft, and just a gut feeling, who we all will care the most about as time marches on. I'm sure we'll be right in some cases, and terribly wrong in others. In the end, the artists themselves, and the decisions they make along the way, create their own destiny.

Now, if you ever see me looking a little wild and all askew, you'll know why it is. I'm working! But hopefully not on television.

And Courtney, or anyone else who cares, the answers to your questions are:

A) I got started in high school. Photography was my hobby.

B) Laying bricks, farming, raising children are hard jobs. Photography is a maddening job. Plus you always have to carry tons of equipment. Plus, you have to have business and artistic skills at the same time. Plus, you have to know and understand computers, and chemistry, and lighting. Plus, you have to make money. Plus . . .

C) You do get to travel to places (but not always when you want to go).

D) I work for myself. Sometimes, magazines (and others) hire me.

E) My advice is: Do what makes you happy. Have faith in yourself. Don't be afraid.

By the way, twenty years from now I plan to do another photo book of country music stars. But in the meanwhile, I truly hope that you enjoy this one!

introduction

by chet flippo

Raeanne Rubenstein has been documenting country music and its makers for over two decades. The images she was creating represented and brought out the creativity of the people she was photographing. You can look at a Rubenstein photograph and hear music. You can look at a Rubenstein photograph and begin to know the country artist you're seeing in a different way. You divine exactly what she is after: to draw out the inner soul of her subject. She uncannily does so.

Her first country music book, *Honkytonk Heroes*, captured the first modern era of country music: the post–Nudie Suit independence movement of a whole new movement in country music. Willie and Waylon and the boys kicked the "Urban Cowboy" crap out of country music and injected a new realism to the music. Now Rubenstein addresses the second wave of modern country, with an eye to ongoing history. Once again, she reaches inside her subjects and pulls out their inner beings.

Gone Country addresses the modern country era, which was born on April 26, 1986, when rangy, earthy Randy Travis's single "On the Other Hand" first charted in *Billboard* and went on to be No. 1. It was the return of raw, honest, real country: but it almost didn't happen. Warner Bros. Records had released the song as a single in August 1985, and it was a relative bomb, rising only to No. 67 in *Billboard*. The second Travis single, "1982," fared better—hitting No. 6—and encouraged Warner Bros. president Jim Ed Norman to try the almost-unprecedented feat of re-releasing "On the Other Hand." That song, with its almost haunted vocal delivery and traditional country themes of temptation and faithfulness, had been considered "too country" (an oxymoronic moniker that is periodically applied to certain country songs) by many country radio stations.

Travis had almost single-handedly come to the rescue of country music. What did it need rescuing from? Well, for one thing, the likes of Marie Osmond and Tom Jones were regularly charting number one on the country charts, with what were not necessarily country songs. In country music's seventy-plus-year history as a readily identifiable form of American popular music, it has periodically gotten itself into dire straits from which it needed to be saved.

Country music has long been a small, insular world with few surprises or deviations from a general mainstream with which both the performers and the audience are comfortable. Its main appeal has always been the fact that it exists as a way of looking at life for a group of people with shared values, life experience, and beliefs. As such, it is viewed as more than just a business, although it is increasingly just and only that for many of its practitioners.

It has always been an intense peer-group music, as timely as tomorrow's headlines and as ageless as the folktales and British and Scottish ballads that helped birth this very peculiarly American music earlier this century.

This is a music that literally forged its own way. It began as homegrown music, performed by neighbors and friends for social gatherings, at church, and at home. As folk music, it remained a private and largely a rural music. It was initially ignored by the music industry, which focused on urban areas. It was dismissed as a possible commercial entity, because it was viewed as "hillbilly" and thus fit only for its own audience—which ironically is what ultimately led to its enormous commercial success. At the time, though, "hillbillies" were not seen as consumers.

World War II was the chief factor in the transformation of country music into the powerful cultural and musical force that it is today. The war marked a massive shift in the United States as much of the rural populace moved to take factory jobs in cities or went into the military and became acclimated to a bigger world. The rural exodus involved both black and white people, and their musics changed as the market and the audience changed. In 1942, *Billboard* hesitantly began covering the musical shift with a column called "Western and Race," lumping what had been rural black and white music together. In 1944 the magazine started a chart listing the "Most Played Juke Box Folk Music Records." "Race" became its own area, and it soon became "Rhythm & Blues." In 1946 the "folk music" chart was changed to the "hillbilly" chart, then was briefly a "folk music" chart again before being dubbed "country & western" which itself became merely "country" in 1962.

The top country artists decade by decade, as monitored by *Billboard* magazine, illustrate country's evolution. The *Billboard* country chart was begun in 1944. Before that, country music was barely recognized as a separate musical genre and distinct commercial market. Once the chart began, the top five performers, tracked decade by decade, were until very recently a fairly stable and cohesive ongoing list. However, a breakdown of the first half of the '90s shows a further mercurial shift as country music audience's attention spans and cycles of artists' popularity grow shorter and shorter:

1940–1949: Eddy Arnold, Ernest Tubb, Bob Wills, Al Dexter, Red Foley

1950–1959: Arnold, Foley, Hank Snow, Carl Smith, Webb Pierce

1960–1969: Arnold, Buck Owens, George Jones, Jim Reeves, Johnny Cash

1970–1979: Conway Twitty, Merle Haggard, Charley Pride, Dolly Parton, Loretta Lynn

1980–1989: Twitty, Haggard, Willie Nelson, Kenny Rogers, Alabama

1990–1993: Alabama, Garth Brooks, George Strait, Reba McEntire, Alan Jackson

1994: McEntire, Jackson, Tim McGraw, John Michael Montgomery, Vince Gill

1995: Montgomery, McGraw, Garth Brooks, Shania Twain, Jeff Foxworthy.

As you can see, longevity used to be the standard for country artists. Eddy Arnold was prominently high up on the charts through three decades, as were many other performers a little further down on the charts. The country audience's loyalty to its stars has—until fairly recently—been a phenomenon unmatched in any other area of popular music. Country music careers were always viewed as tenured for life.

A visit to Fan Fair, the big love fest between country artists and country fans that the Country Music Association puts on every summer at the Tennessee State Fairgrounds in Nashville, offers an object lesson. Tens of thousands of fans from around the country and the world literally plan their summers around a visit to Nashville to commune with their musical idols. And it does become a love fest. Most prominent country performers give up a week of their lucrative summer bookings (of state fairs, festivals, and the likes) to perform for free at Fan Fair. They sit in elaborately decorated booths to meet and greet their fans for hours on end, signing endless autographs, and pressing the flesh of the people who keep their careers alive. This kind of intimate association is unique to country music.

At 1996's Fan Fair, Garth Brooks made an unannounced visit and—before he could even get to a booth—was trapped outside an exhibition hall by the press of fans; he ended up standing in place and signing autographs for 23 hours without stopping: or eating or drinking or doing anything else. Brooks is now the best-selling solo recording artist in the history of recorded popular music but he wisely knows that he needs to retain that loyal fan base and—perhaps even more importantly—needs to maintain the perception that that fan base is all-important to him.

That's what nurtured country music since the early days, when all performers were literally your neighbors or your fellow churchgoers who happened to have a little musical talent. This, after all, was a music that began as a very uncommercial art form, folk music performed by the immigrants to the South from the United Kingdom. It literally was parlor entertainment, dance music, and church hymns. When country music eventually began to become a commercial music, in the 1920s, it still was a peer-group music, very much identified as rural, string-band music. In the 1930s, the mainstream of country music was true hillbilly music, simultaneously mournful and celebratory music of life in the mountains in the Southeast. In the 1940s, as the rural populace headed for the big cities and factory jobs, honky-tonk music took over. It was electrified for the first time—to be heard above the din of the crowds in the frenzied honky-tonks—and the themes exemplified the homesickness for the old home place left behind and also the lure of the new urban attractions of dim lights, thick smoke, and loud music in the tonks: and of cheating, the seduction of adultery in those dim clubs.

As more and more rural folk moved to the cities, a second generation of country music fan began to turn away from the rawer sounds of the honky-tonks, and the smooth sound of "countrypolitan" music was born. That developed into the even smoother "Nashville Sound" that Chet Atkins perfected in Nashville. The next generation of fan rebelled against all that smoothness and flocked to the rough-hewn "Outlaw" music of the likes of Willie Nelson and Waylon Jennings. Then, that sound and look was co-opted into the smoother "Urban Cowboy" movement, spawned by the hit movie of the same name. George Strait led a heroic attack against the Urban Cowboy sound, and Randy Travis and a whole flock of other traditionalists turned country back to a straighter, simpler path. The so-called Class of '89, represented by class leaders Garth Brooks and Alan Jackson, not only strengthened the traditionalists' hold on the genre, they attracted outside listeners from the rock and pop audiences. Soon, country artists were regularly selling albums in platinum numbers, and Garth Brooks started selling in the tens of millions.

Nothing succeeds like success, and Nashville was soon caught up in an unparalleled growth. For a while, in the early 1990s, everything "country" sold, and the gold (and platinum) rush was on. A town with ten country music record labels in 1990 sported 27 by 1995. Sales went from $750 million in 1990 to $2 billion in 1995. Because so much of the new country audience was young, the record labels looked for youth and looks in their new performers, and what had once been a very stable group of country music artists became a shifting tableau, an uneasy mix of youth and fading beauty. 1996 saw a slight downturn in country sales and the industry began to react to what had obviously become a case of oversaturation of the market. At the same time, the notion of what was "commercial country music" began to shift, as such young mavericks as Lyle Lovett and the Mavericks made inroads on traditional country radio, and veterans such as Johnny Cash and

Rodney Crowell—representing two generations of country pioneers rejected by the mainstream country music industry—forged new audiences of alternative country music fans.

Country music and portraiture have enjoyed a long and friendly, if not always intimate relationship. The very nature of country music and its singers and musicians—a frankness and openness and embrace of its audience—would seem to ensure an intimacy with photography. There has traditionally never been a wall between country performers and their audience, so why should there be one between the performer and the camera? And to be sure, there have been marvelous examples of inspired portraiture of country artists from the first, showing the very candid nature of the music and its makers.

Initially, the country music portrait was a very formal affair, as all portraiture was in the first decades of this century. Having a portrait taken (or "made" in the parlance of the time) was, for the working men and women of the South, a rare occasion, and it usually marked a formal event, a wedding or family reunion or other solemn occasion (portraits of the dead were still being taken then). And, given the nature of the technology of contemporary photography, the portrait session itself was an event of a solemn nature. The bulky studio view cameras and their lengthy exposure times necessitated that the person posing for the portrait had to sit very still indeed—many photographers still used the neck braces that lingered from the Daguerreotype era. Those braces literally embraced the sitter's neck in a vice-like clamp. Not surprisingly, then, those of us viewing photographs from that era have always considered our forbears to be grim, silent, and tight-lipped people, joyless in their formal, bulky, and dark clothing.

The earliest portraits of country musicians, then, tend to show rigid, unsmiling, almost vacant-eyed people who clearly are not enjoying life. I remember seeing one of the first portraits of the Carter Family, taken in the 1920s. They are dressed in their finest: A. P. Carter wears a dark suit, white shirt, and dark tie, and Sara and Maybelle are in matching high-necked dresses and capes. Of course, that was also their stage dress. And, to be certain that they were identified as musicians in the portrait, Maybelle holds her arch-topped guitar and Sara grips her autoharp. All three are grim and tense and look as if they have just returned from a funeral.

Country artists performed in their finest clothes (except for those few, mostly string bands, who traded on a hillbilly image and sported overalls, or the occasional cowboy performer from out West, and many of them still wore business suits). A 1930 publicity portrait shows an unsmiling Gene Autry in dark suit and tie, long before he assumed his trademark cowboy garb. Vernon Dalhart wore a tuxedo in his portraits, and Cliff Carlisle sported a three-piece checked suit with a white handkerchief in his pocket. The era of flashy stage costumes would not come for decades.

It should also be remembered that country performers' portraits were taken for publicity purposes, to go on handbills and advertisements for their live appearances, as well as on the sheet music of their songs. Therefore, the performers were at the mercy of whatever portrait studio they entrusted with their image. This began to change when performers on radio station WLS's "National Barn Dance" in the 1930s were sent to the "Theatrical Chicago" studio; the results were a dramatic and marked departure for country portraits. The portraits are less formal, artfully posed tableaux that are much livelier than pictures had been. Lulu Belle and Scotty wear colorful outfits and are actually smiling as they play guitar and banjo. They are shown full-length, rather than the traditional head-and-shoulder shot. Wavy-haired Bradley Kincaid gets a bit of the Vaseline treatment for a gauzy glamour shot, which also was unusual. A young George Gobel wears a cowboy outfit and holds his ukulele in a dramatically shadowed, lit-from-below portrait. The Three Little Maids have their marcelled hair highlighted from above. An element of humor even crept in: the Hoosier Hot Shots were portrayed helplessly ensnared in a pile of their musical instruments.

Country music's image (and of course its portraits) were forever changed in the 1940s by an unlikely outside force. That force has been little studied and a word or two about it is called for. A Brooklyn-born hustler named Nudie Cohen, who had been a boxer, run a dry cleaners, and sewn pasties and G-strings for burlesque houses in New York, decided to try his luck making movie costumes in Hollywood. He made friends with western singer Tex Williams, who loaned him $150 for a sewing machine with which to set up shop. Nudie studied the outfits in the singing cowboy movies and decided that country and western singers ought to dress up like that, too. His theory was that the singers owed it to their audiences to dress up and offer some glamour and fantasy. Tex Williams tried out some of Nudie's outfits—which came to be known as "Nudie Suits"—and discovered that he not only liked them, but his audiences did, too. Nudie combined movie star cowboy outfits with a little costume jewelry, fancy piping, sequins and rhinestones, two-and-three-tone boots with elaborate designs, and fancy hats.

Hank Williams discovered Nudie when he was in Hollywood for a screen test with Dore Schary, and he fell in love with Nudie Suits and introduced the look to Nashville. Some of Nudie's outfits were conservative: a tan western gabardine with piping was his version of the blue serge business suit for country artists. Others were more elaborate. Hank's "Lovesick Blues" suit had the musical notes of that song embroidered in black on the white suit. "Taste" was not a word heard often in the fitting rooms of Nudie's North Hollywood shop and his imagination ran wild. The sequin-and-rhinestone designs ran to rampant lengths: from Porter Wagoner's wagon-wheel outfit in the 1960s to Gram Parsons' marijuana-leaf decorated suit in the 1970s, Nudie changed the look of country music. (Although Nudie is dead, his apprentice, known only as "Manuel," continues to garb country stars from a tailor shop and showroom on Broadway in Nashville. It's called, of course, "Manuel's.")

When the Nudie Suit look hit Nashville, glamour became a staple in country portraiture. Those performers who wore Nudie suits wanted to be shown to high effect in their portraits, and those who didn't wear them wanted to look just as glamorous. A collection of portraits from the 1950s and 1960s shows Hank Snow dramatically backlit in his white Nudie Suit and Mel Tillis cradling his chin pensively (mood shots!) in his red Nudie Suit. Others are no less dramatic: Willie Nelson lit from under his chin, and Minnie Pearl looking very thoughtful in bright light and shadow. Country music's image became highly stylized.

There were other factors at work in the symbiosis between country music and portraiture. The image of country was forever altered by the introduction of long-playing phonograph albums (LPs) in 1947. As LPs became popular in country music, the logical thing to do was to put a portrait of the artist on his or her album cover, rather than the early practice of using graphics. In the competition in retail store bins, a distinctive album cover obviously had the edge in attracting the customer's attention. By and large, LP covers were unimaginative head-shot portraits, but the demand was there and photographers rushed to meet it.

The other factor was country music's growing success and, simultaneously, the media's acceptance of it. Throughout country music's history, it had been considered by most magazines and newspapers, and TV and radio, as unworthy of coverage. It might exist, but it did not do so in the living rooms of decent, upright citizens. As recently as the 1960s, country stars did not usually get their names in the newspaper, unless they were arrested or died. Magazines ignored country music altogether. (The same situation later existed for rock music, but the cycle was considerably shorter there.)

As country became more popular and acceptable, the media began to cover it more fully, resulting in a need for more country artists' images. Portraits met the need. More photographers were attracted to country music but that quantitative change did not necessarily result in a qualitative one. Just as the boom in country music has drawn many opportunists to Nashville who do not necessarily know and understand the music, many photographers were drawn to Music City for commercial reasons. You can tell by the portraits which photographers intuit country music and which are simply looking for images to sell. I have seen savvy country artists shuck and jive and manipulate naive but ambitious photographers into getting what they want many times.

Country singers by and large can gauge pretty quickly when a journalist or a photographer doesn't understand their music, and they act accordingly: a shallow article or a shallow photograph is the result. It's all about empathy on the part of the photographer and trust on the part of the country singer. Empathy and trust are rare, and there's a tiny handful of photographers working today in all of music photography who are privy to both.

Raeanne Rubenstein is one of them. Consider a few of her images: Tanya Tucker dancing free in the woods; Rodney Crowell as wood nymph; Martina McBride caught in a mirror; Barbara Mandrell as Catwoman; Ty Herndon pushed into a corner; Joe Diffie as Prometheus; Johnny Cash as Mount Rushmore; Randy Travis opening his shirt up and becoming soap opera material; Hank Williams Jr. with his favorite flintlock rifle; Michael Martin Murphey becoming Buffalo Bill; BR5-49 bonding with a barroom; Marty Stuart showing off as consummate Nudie/Manuel Suit wearer; Marshall Chapman's silent scream; Merle Haggard telling a riotous story in a series of takes; George Jones upstaging singing partner Tammy Wynette as stand-up comedian; 14-year-old phenomenon LeAnn Rimes posing first sticking her tongue out as a teenager and then shown coiled like a seductive cat; spike-haired and gamin-eyed Shelby Lynn pulling down her pants for a reason; Eddie Rabbitt merging with nature; William Lee Golden becoming part of the forest; Mark Collie as part of the hay harvest; the Sweethearts of the Rodeo as proud Indian princesses with their horses; and Lee Roy Parnell as Rhett Butler. The other thing about Raeanne Rubenstein that I want to tell you about is that her work inspires you to look through the frame of the photograph, to catch a glimpse of what's going on beyond the frame of the portrait. There's a lot happening there.

I can usually look at a Rubenstein portrait and see the tableau unfolding there, and hear the dialogue, listen to the music, and sense the unseen. Portraiture into the very soul of a music is very rare. That's especially problematic in a music as eclectic as country music.

Sometimes country music swaggers, sometimes it swears, sometimes it roars, again it carries a briefcase and speaks in clipped tones, or it murmurs or purrs or wanders all over creation. Cameras can't keep up with it.

Recall when it was trendy for photographers to try to actually photograph music itself? Or, at the very least, to capture the sense and sweep of music on film? It was a very laudable, if perhaps ill-considered proposition. The results ranged from predictable to startling. One very famous photographer tried to depict a symphony orchestra's crescendos by superimposing images of the orchestra itself building upwards: a stairway to heaven, as it were. Another photographer almost worried himself to death trying to depict jazz's erratic grandeur through a series of blurred motion studies of performers and their musical instruments: enter sax at left; exit trumpet stage right. Movement itself does not intrinsically paint music, but the impulse is very basic: watch at any rock, country, jazz, or bluegrass concert—even without listening, *especially* without listening—and you can tell when the music is building to a climax. That's when the amateur photographers rush the stage and the flashes start blinking.

I feel that these photographers are missing the point: the closest that you can come to understanding music through images is by confronting the very face of music itself. And that, of course, is by looking into and through the face and eyes of the creator of the music into the very soul.

The odds are very good that when you look at Rubenstein's photographs, you begin to hear a melody. Rodney Crowell through Raeanne Rubenstein's eye is a creator of the kind of music that you suspect he must create. The same applies to everyone on whom she turns her discerning eye. It's because she listens and understands—and then captures and translates.

the photos

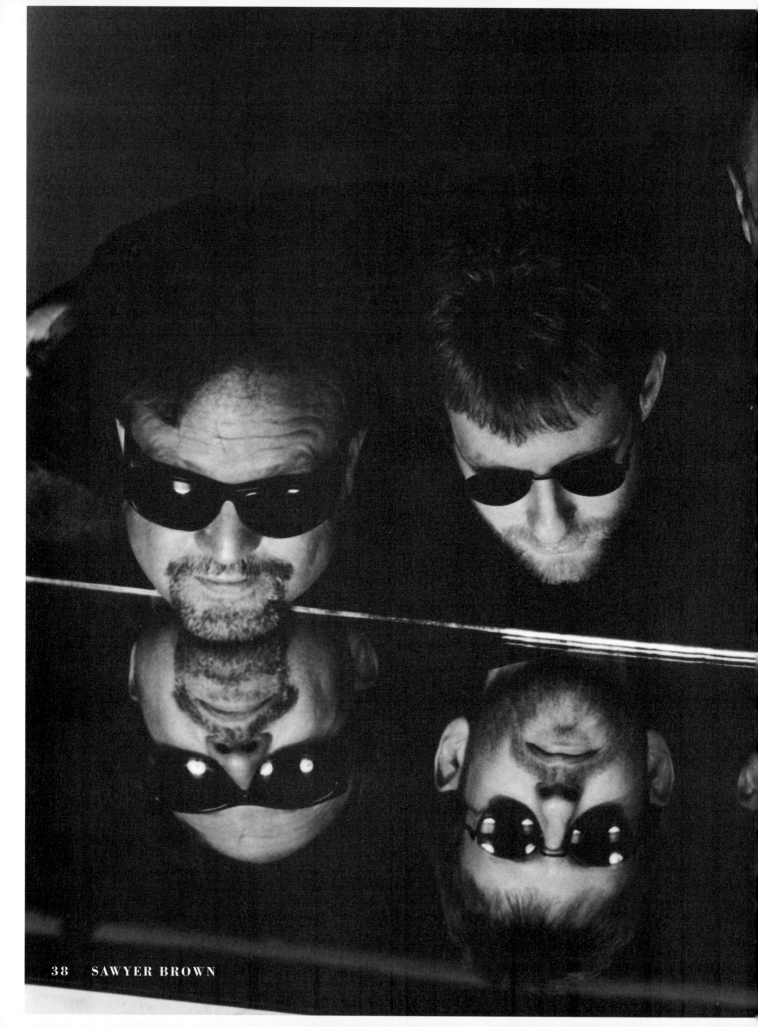

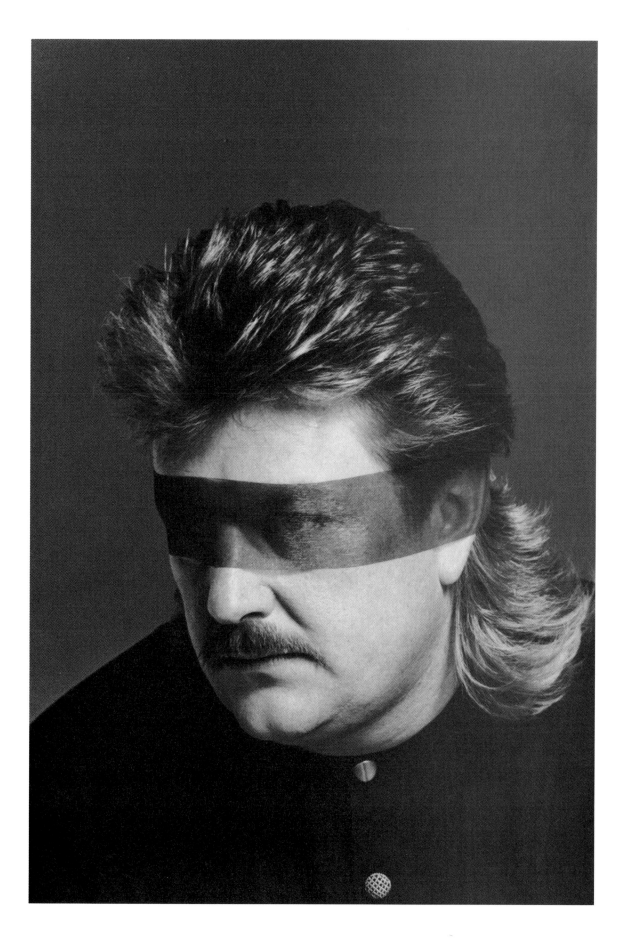

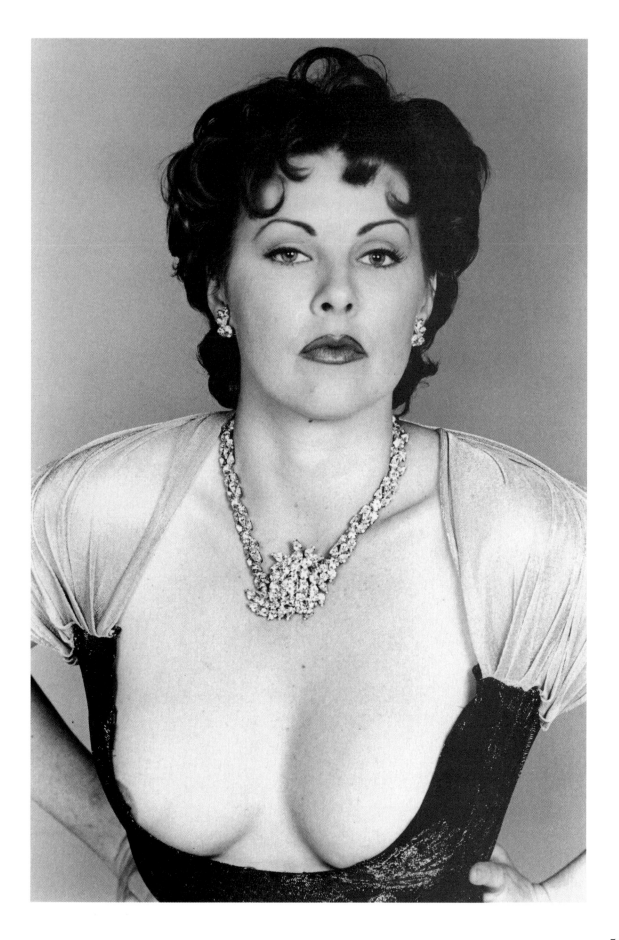

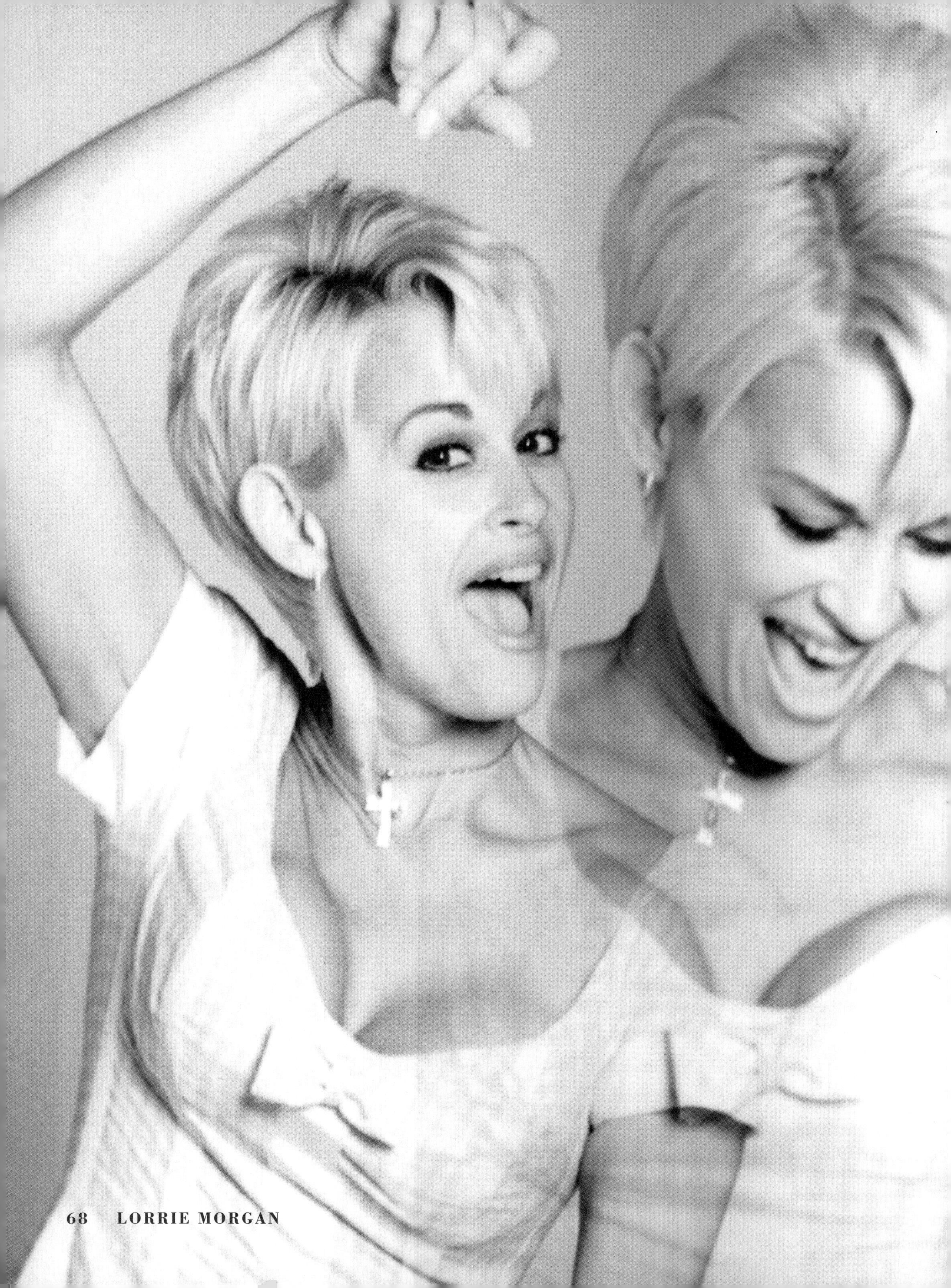

DANNY FRAZIER

HANK WILLIAMS, JR.   79

98   FAITH HILL

101

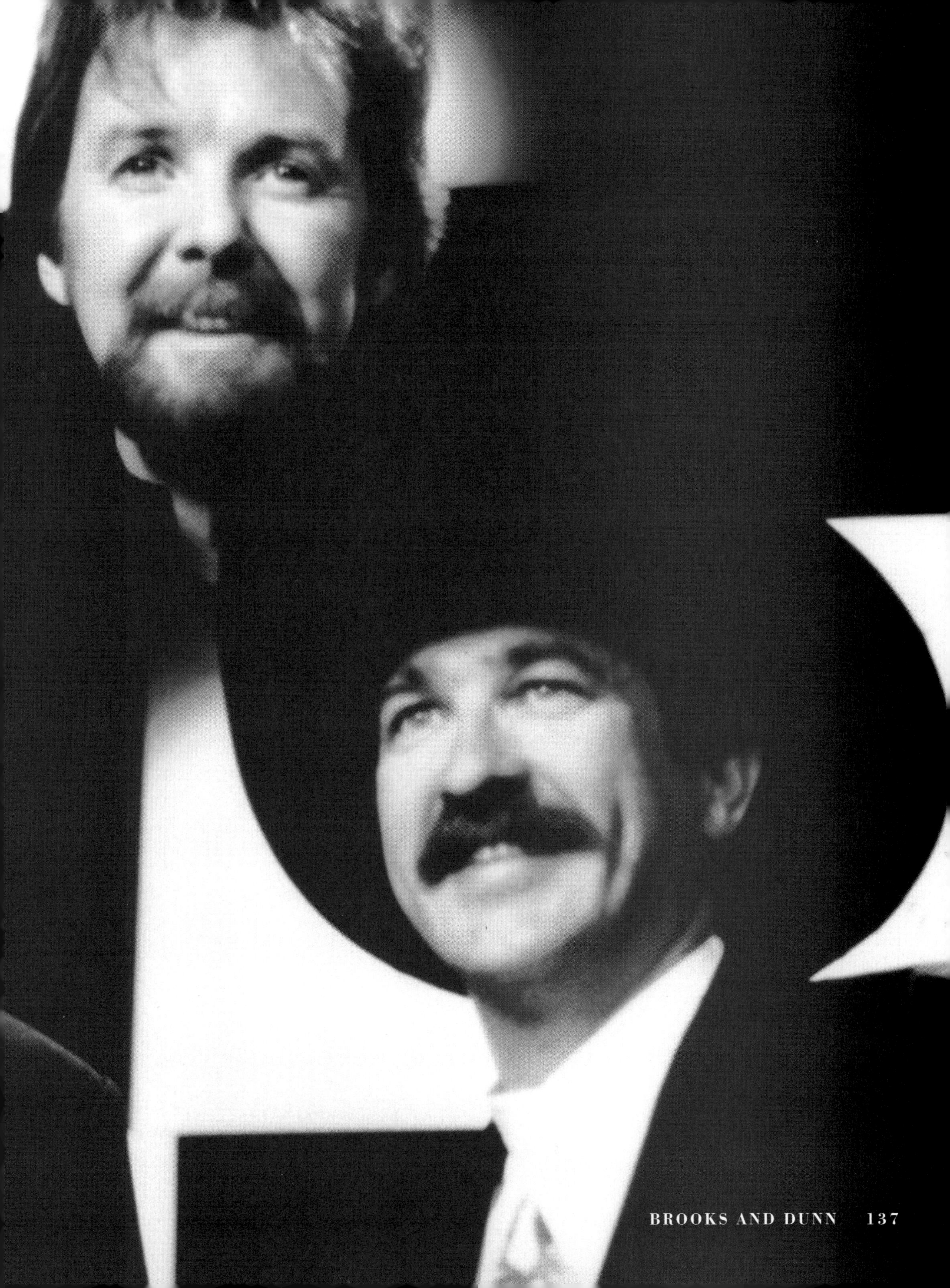

148 **REBA McENTIRE**

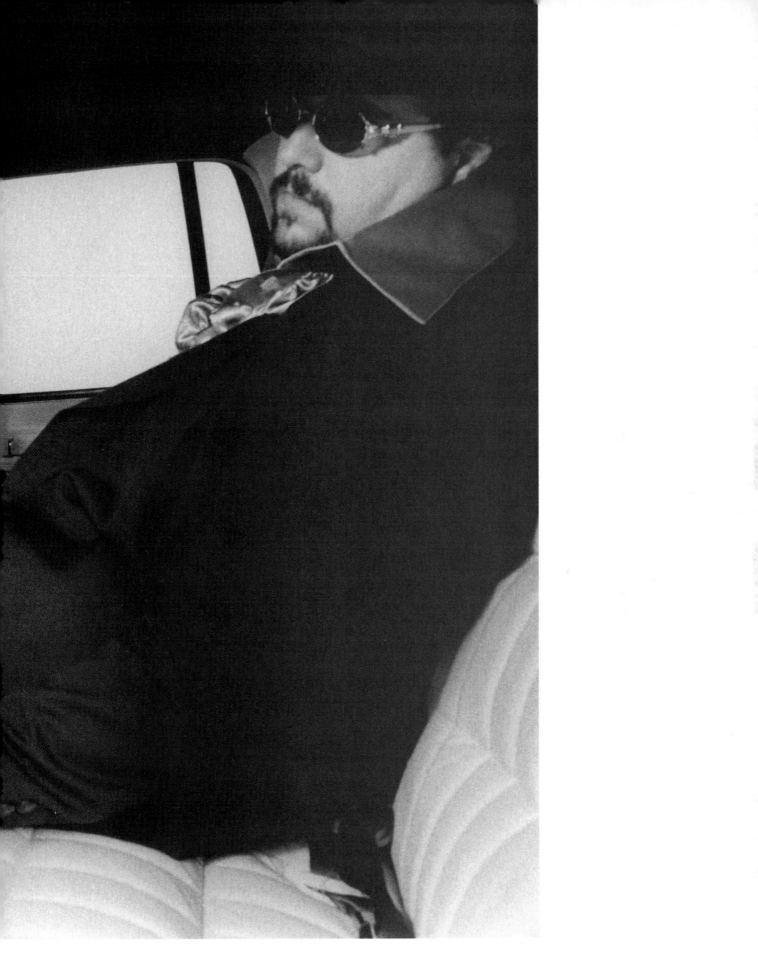

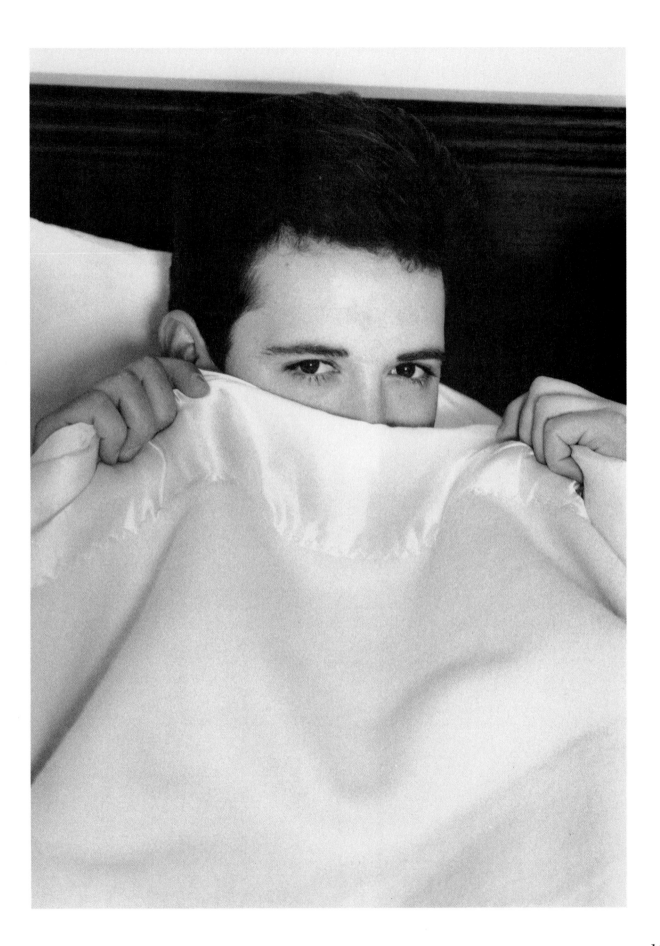

captions

30/31 MARK CHESNUTT

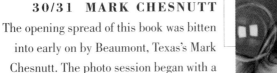

The opening spread of this book was bitten into early on by Beaumont, Texas's Mark Chesnutt. The photo session began with a serious tone, Mark, dark, brooding, in black leather. But no sooner did he discover the bubble bottle I had brought to entertain his baby son, Waylon, than he was launched into this funny, wacky series of shots. Often enough, the best-laid plans make way for serendipity.

35 TIM McGRAW

This simple portrait of Tim McGraw was taken in the blink of an eye, backstage at an arena in Savannah, Georgia. He was on tour with Faith Hill as his opening act and, for some reason, he preferred to hang with her instead of me.

38/39 SAWYER BROWN

Photographing a band is always a challenge, because bands have a tendency to look alike. My ambition is for every artist to look unique. I like to use mirrors in photos when it's appropriate, and I felt that Sawyer Brown required the very dramatic treatment a mirror could provide. This narrow mirror came off the bathroom wall in the studio, and I shot it from the ceiling, 20 feet up.

41 THE LYNNS
Twins Peggy and Patsy are country royalty to the max. The heirs apparent of country music queen Loretta Lynn and her late husband, Mooney, they recently got together as a musical duo.

32/33/34 MARTINA McBRIDE

Martina arrived at the studio late, having just gotten off the road. She also felt unprepared, because she hadn't really thought about what she wanted to do. However, I knew I wanted Martina to look very hip and modern. The images you see here turned out to be the perfect spontaneous collaboration between the makeup artist, Mary Beth Felts, me (I thought of using the mirror), and Martina, who came up with the "I see you" message. The moustache was my idea, but Marybeth had to draw it, and Martina, of course, had to wear it.

36/37 TOBY KEITH
Toby is a former semi-pro football star, who's now a country star. He's large, very masculine, and for some reason makes me think of statues of the Greek God Zeus. I call these pictures the "Toby on high" series.

40 CLINT BLACK
One of the most prominent of the Gone Hollywood country types, Clint still wears his hat, symbolic of his Texas, honky-tonkin' roots.

42/43 BARBARA MANDRELL

Although it took many months to arrange this photo shoot with Barbara Mandrell, when it finally happened Barbara gave it her all! We took pictures from morning until late at night, trying different things, experimenting. It was my concept to focus on the classic, sexy side of this versatile woman. Her new goal is to go Hollywod as an actress. I'd be looking for her there!

44 NEAL McCOY

Shot backstage in a portable studio at the Opry, Neal was in a raucous mood during this shoot! He laughed and giggled and clowned around. This picture captures him in a more serious moment.

45 JOE DIFFIE

Marty Stuart told me he thought this picture was scary. I think it's mysterious. Joe may sing humorous, honky-tonk songs, but I think there's a lot more going on there than meets the eye.

46/47 SHANIA TWAIN

Long overdue, Shania is the pop goddess of current country. With a unique sound, sexy good looks, and a pro-woman message in her songs, everyone loves her. These pictures were taken at Nashville's Fan Fair.

48/49 CHET ATKINS

Legendary guitarist Chet Atkins never quits! I've seen him perform more in the last six months than ever before. This picture of Chet was taken in his office, on the second floor of a beautiful old house on Music Row. The picture that he's holding, a copy of his original publicity still dating from 1942, was inscribed for me. He wrote, "For Raeanne, When I was young, Chet Atkins."

50/51/52 RODNEY CROWELL

Rodney Crowell is a delightful rogue doing things his own way, for better or worse. Before this photo shoot, I spoke to Rodney directly, something that doesn't happen very often. I wanted to know if there was a fantasy image floating around in his mind that I might be able to work with. His simple response was, "Well, I like water." With that as my cue, I went searching for what I thought was appropriate water for Rodney Crowell, and ended up finding it in the form of a waterfall far down the Natchez Trace, about 50 miles from Nashville.

53 MARTY ROE OF DIAMOND RIO

This picture was taken after the Diamond Rio Celebrity Golf Tournament, an annual charity event. Although I've photographed Diamond Rio several times since this picture was taken, it's my favorite (love that tree!).

54/55 TY HERNDON

1995 was a tough year for Ty, a year in which he was forced to face up to some personal problems he had in his life in a very public way. I feel that Ty is a survivor, and has the fortitude to overcome. That is what I had in mind when I photographed him emerging from a box (of his own making).

56/57 BOBBIE CRYNER

Bobbie Cryner looks like a silent screen goddess, an effect amplified by these gowns she made. Sexy and daring, Bobbie's career has been filled with dramatic highs and lows, a pattern not likely to change any time soon.

58 GUY CLARK

I first met Guy Clark at the Willie Nelson Picnic in 1974. At the time he was a lanky Texan in a cowboy hat. Along with his wife and muse, painter Susanna Clark, they are wild things cutting a wide swath through the Nashville songwriting community. I never heard a Guy Clark song I didn't like, and his recent CD, *Dublin Blues*, is a favorite. I've always thought Guy lives on a different plane from the rest of us, so lo and behold there is a glimpse of it, in the upper right corner of this frame.

59 K. T. OSLIN

I was present while KT was being interviewed about her life for the last five years. She spoke about her health, her quadruple bypass heart operation, her fear and her longings, but above all about her new record, the first in five years, appropriately called *My Roots Are Showing*, a collection of country jazzy songs from the '30s and '40s that she delivers in classy KT style. The cover image shows her naked behind a large feather fan, very wacky, very fun.

60 DOUG STONE

This is Doug Stone in all his sartorial splendor, camping it up at the T. J. Martell Foundation Music City Celebrity Fashion Show during Fan Fair week.

61 KEN MELLONS

This picture was a collaboration between Ken, (the washtub was his Grandma's, and the juke-box junkie books are his), Sony Records (who produced the rubber duck to promote his album), and me (who provided the towel).

62 JAMES HOUSE

James House is one of the edgier country artists, visually more on the pop than country side. His blonde good looks and his fun-loving spirit make him a favorite of mine. Go, James!

63 PAM TILLIS

This cute picture of Pam in pigtails was taken at her Fan Fair booth.

64/65 THE "GRAND OLE OPRY" CAST

This delightful shot of the legends of the Grand Ole Opry is a rarity. It was taken on a Friday night, between the two radio broadcasts. I'm proud to have been able to include (top) Bill Anderson (an Opry member since 1950), Stonewall Jackson (1969), Porter Wagonner (1957), Del Reeves (1966), Jeannie Seely (1967), Johnny Russell (1985), Jimmy C. Newman (1956); (bottom) Jack Greene (1967), Little Jimmy Dickens (1948), Grandpa Jones (1947), Skeeter Davis (1959); (seated) Jeannie Pruett (1973). Other members of the Opry appearing in this book include Garth Brooks, Vince Gill, Marty Stuart, Alan Jackson, Martina McBride, George Jones, Alison Krauss, Barbara Mandrell, Joe Diffie, Lorrie Morgan, Emmylou Harris, Charlie Pride, Ricky Van Shelton, Holly Dunn, and Steve Wariner.

66 JOHN ANDERSON

One of the so-called New Traditionalists, John Anderson appears and disappears from the charts. Here, he's laughing at some of my stories.

67/68/69 LORRIE MORGAN

I was invited to photograph Lorrie Morgan at a rehearsal studio in Nashville. She was there to rehearse "Don't Worry Baby," which she recorded with the song's originators, the Beach Boys, as part of a tribute album. I set up a portable studio, Lorrie walked over, and just as she was ready to pose, the actual Beach Boys began to rehearse "Fun Fun Fun" and "Little Deuce Coupe" as Lorrie danced along. It was an amazing experience to have the Beach Boys, live and in person, performing as the studio background music.

70 DANNY FRAZIER

Danny Frazier was lead singer of Frazier River and a native Texan. He plans to tour as a solo act in 1997.

71 JOHNNY CASH

This portrait was taken backstage at the taping of "The Marty Party," Marty Stuart's TV program appearing on TNN.

72 RANDY TRAVIS

Randy Travis's original, 1986 success is the demarcation point for what this book is calling "New Country." The original "New Traditionist," Randy brought an honesty and genuine country-sounding approach back to country music. Discovered by bar owner/Svengali Lib Hatcher at age 16, she managed him and supported his career for many years. They are now married (mighty, but tiny, blonde-haired Lib attended this photo shoot).

73 SUZY BOGGUSS
This shot was taken just before dark one summer afternoon in Suzy's backyard. It is one of my all-time favorites.

74 MICKEY GILLEY AND GLEN CAMPBELL
I drove from Nashville, through the Ozark Mountains to Branson, Missouri for this shot, taken early one morning outside the Mickey Gilley Theatre on the infamous parking lot known as Highway 76. Afterward, we heard that traffic was backed up for miles.

75 CHARLIE PRIDE
Charlie Pride was tired and pensive the day I returned to Branson to do this portrait of him. We had a very deep and philosophical conversation about the meaning of life/love/success. This picture was taken in his dressing room at the Charlie Pride Theatre.

76/77 THE PRESLEYS
Reputedly the "first family of Branson," they opened their "Presleys' Mountain Music Jubilee" in 1967. There are three generations of Presleys in this picture, all of whom perform in the family business. Steve Presleys' (third from the left) wife's name is Raeanne, same as mine, and the only other Raeanne that I've ever met.

78/79 HANK WILLIAMS, JR.
Hank is a wild man, who puts on raucous rock-and-roll style country concerts that drive his many loyal fans wild. He loves to hunt and fish, and lives way out in the country in remote Paris, Tennessee. The gun he is carrying is part of his extensive gun collection, of which he is extremely proud, and which includes items as big as original Gatling guns, to small Civil War bullets he's found himself.

80/81 SHELTON HANK WILLIAMS III
Shelton is the son of Hank, Jr. and grandson of the original Hank Williams, but believe it or not, he's been a well-kept secret. Almost no one yet knows that he's given up rock and roll and returned to his country roots. As these pictures clearly show, his resemblance to his grandfather (the original Hank Williams died at the young age of 29) is uncanny. If he shares the musical gifts that run in his family, Hank Williams III should be a star.

82 TRACY LAWRENCE
As Atlantic Records' new, young hitmaker, Tracy has presence and swagger. This photo session took place in a hallway, converted to a lunchroom, converted to a photo studio for an hour, after a press conference, before a rehearsal for a TV taping ("A Tribute to Conway Twitty"), that was before a John Michael Montgomery album release party. Tracy is a busy man.

83 DOLLY PARTON

After the CMA Award Show, looking great.

84 RICKY VAN SHELTON

People may not realize that Ricky Van has many interests apart fom music. He has written a series of children's books (Quacker is the main character) and he flies his own plane. This picture was taken one morning at the crack of dawn at the Lebanon, Tennessee, airport, as he was preparing to fly off in his plane, there behind him.

85 EDDIE RABBITT

I couldn't resist trying to do the rabbit thing with Eddie. I went to a costume shop and bought the little ears, and then I went to his classicly restored home in Williamson County. In his historically correct, elegantly furnished living room, I pulled out my ears and asked him if he'd wear them. "I'll do anything rabbit," he said.

86/87 TERRI CLARK

I shot these pictures of our cover girl Terri Clark, playing air guitar on a mountainside in Copper Mountain, Colorado. She was appearing at West Fest, Michael Martin Murphey's annual festival of country music, and Indian and cowboy culture. At the time, her first single was #6 with a bullet and she was hoping for a big hit. With several #1s now under her belt, the girl in the hat is launched.

88 RICK TREVINO

Tejano country star Rick Trevino went natural for this photo, grabbing a quick drink from this mountain stream in Colorado.

89 AMY GRANT

Gospel singer, beautiful woman, wife of Gary Chapman, mother—and she can really whack that golf ball.

90/91 ALABAMA

Based in Birmingham, Alabama's amazingly successful career has survived through two decades, no mean feat in the country climate of today. These individual portraits capture the four unique "faces" of the band.

92/93 HOLLY DUNN

These pictures of beautiful Holly Dunn were shot in the empty studio B at the Grand Ole Opry. Behind Holly, on page 93, is my portable studio set-up, in case you were wondering what it looked like.

96/97 DOUG SUPERNAW

The long tall Texan Doug Supernaw was fun to shoot. Willing to do almost anything, during this shoot Doug chased a horse, hung upside down from a swing set, took off his clothes, jumped in a pool, and otherwise did whatever I asked. He later told people about this session, "I stoned him with my mind" and perhaps I did.

100/101 ALAN JACKSON

Although Alan Jackson is famous for avoiding the press whenever possible, he agreed to sit for these simple portraits for me. The title of this book, "Gone Country" is also the title of his huge country hit song, so I'm especially glad to have such cool pictures of him.

103 DWIGHT YOAKAM

Dwight Yoakam, young, hip, a Kentuckian transplanted to Los Angeles, in his best "Nudie"-style garb.

94/95 STEVE WARINER

Wariner is a mentor to many of Nashville's young artists, Brian White prominently among them. I shot this picture at night, outside, in front of Steve's house. We kept hearing this rustling sound coming from the tree behind him, and ever since have argued whether it was bats (me) or birds (Steve) making the eerie noises.

98/99 FAITH HILL

Faith Hill wore a black leather cat suit the night I saw her appear in Savannah. Pretty far out for country, I thought. But then, Faith is from the new young pop/country mode that most definitely includes Shania Twain, and her new husband, Tim McGraw, who wore black satin and a cowboy hat the same night. Here, Faith played softball at a City of Hope charity event during Fan Fair week.

102 MICHAEL MARTIN MURPHEY

I met Michael many years ago, when I went to Taos, New Mexico, to photograph him at home for *People Magazine*. At the time, he was a "country" singer. When I saw him again, all these years later, he told me that article had changed his life, because the writer had referred to him as a "Cowboy" singer, the first time he realized, he said, that that was really what he wanted to be. This photo of him in his "Wild Bill" garb, was taken at Copper Mountain, Colorado during his annual Labor Day festival called Westfest.

104/105 BR5-49 After years as the house band at Robert's Western Wear, a small, funky club located near Tootsie's Orchid Lounge in downtown Nashville, this band has just been signed to Arista, a major label. Now, they tour constantly and can rarely be seen at Robert's. They did however put in an appearance there for me. By the way, their name is taken from an old-time phone number on Junior Sample's skit from "Hee Haw."

106 MARTY STUART I cannot say enough good things about Marty Stuart, singer, picker, songwriter, country historian, collector, artist, and photographer. If he wasn't so young, he'd be the grand old man of Nashville.

107 TRAVIS TRITT When Travis came to the studio for his portrait session, he wore his signature tight-leather pants and fringe, but he was no T-R-O-U-B-L-E at all.

108/109 MARTY STUART Marty stopped by the studio one day to visit. We talked about this and that, including what we should do for his portrait for this book. We thought of several complicated ideas, which we both liked. Suddenly, inspiration struck, and he said, "Grab your camera," and headed outside on a cold, blustery February day. We found the tire laying in the gutter, and Marty did the rest.

110/111 CHRIS LeDOUX I had the foresight to bring some rope to the studio on the day of the Chris Ledoux shoot. I thought it would make a great prop for the country singer and artist. I was right, because he knows roping from his many years in the rodeo.

112 LEE ROY PARNELL I like this picture because of the horse on one side and the TV on the other, symbols to me of old and new country. Lee Roy looks like a rough-and-tumble plantation owner, circa 1850, with flaming red hair, perfect for this portrait.

113 BRYAN WHITE This photo was taken at RCA Studio B, where so many legendary country hits have been recorded. Brian's publicist pointed out that Brian has often been compared to the young Elvis. This is Brian White's Elvis imitation.

114 HERB JEFFRIES

Herb was a singing cowboy in B-westerns during the '30s. Like Roy Rogers and Gene Autrey, he rose to great heights in the movies, in his case as the first and greatest black singing cowboy.

115 THE THOMPSON BROTHERS
This comic photo of new artists The Thompson Brothers should give audiences a taste of the unique experience in store. Watch for them!

116/117 VINCE GILL
One-time country demo singer, Vince is among the most popular, and most generous, donor of time to charitable causes of any country music artist. The music community has paid its respect to him by inviting Vince to host the prestigious Country Music Award show for the past several years.

118/119/120/121 GARTH BROOKS
Brooks is reputed to have sold more records than any recording artist in any musical genre except the Beatles. He does some amazing things, including the marathon 23-hour autograph session he gave to his fans at the 1996 Fan Fair. These amazing portraits were taken on that occasion. The portrait of Garth on page 121 is one of my favorites.

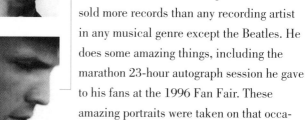

122/123 MARSHALL CHAPMAN
Marshall has been a friend for 20 years. I did her album cover in 1975 and when we reunited, I did her CD cover in 1996. Through the years she has put herself through many trials, as so many artists do, but, lucky for her, and thanks to her tremendous spirit and zest for life, she has overcome them all. These photos are in tribute to her, and to all women who overcome their personal demons.

126/127 MERLE HAGGARD
Words just can't describe Merle Haggard. Although he's known to be temperamental, independent, and unreliable, on this particular day he was a dream subject for me, cooperative and fun. The portrait was taken on a grand staircase at the back of the Ryman, and the one on the right, which I call "Merle Tells a Story," was taken in his dressing room, where he spent hours swapping stories with his pals.

124/125 LITTLE TEXAS
Voted by me as the handsomest band at the City of Hope charity softball game.

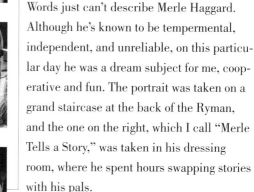

128/129 EMMYLOU HARRIS

Emmylou's recent CD, *Wrecking Ball*, is an artist's Declaration of Independence. It inspires me to be fearless and to go forward. During our photo shoot, I asked Emmy how often she gets photographed in a year, and she said only once, much to my surprise. She said the relationship, the comfort level she has with a photographer is more important to her than their work. Emmylou's a fan of photography, especially Henri Cartier Bresson.

130/131 WYNONNA

Shot backstage during a video taping, Wynonna and I had fun as she mimicked some old-timey movie stills.

132 BILLY RAY CYRUS

Billy Ray is a controversial figure in Nashville. Some people seem to think he didn't work hard enough for his phenomenal success, that it was too much, too soon. I don't know. Although I'm not a fan of "Achy, Breaky Heart" I'm a huge fan of *Songs from the Heartland*, which I listen to all the time, especially "One Last Look." More people came to Billy Ray's Fan Fair breakfast than almost any other artist (over 1,600 people, I was told), and he puts on a killer show.

133/134/135 TANYA TUCKER

When Tanya Tucker started her career, I was there. I did a publicity session with her on the streets of Manhattan when she was still at CBS Records. She was 14 at the time. I photographed her again when she was 16, at a birthday party MCA Records had for her in an amusement park (they rented the whole place, and gave her a car as birthday gift). I photographed her again at Farm Aid in 1985 (she had grown up by then), but I hadn't seen her since. When this photo session was scheduled, I was delighted, because I was anxious to see what had become of my little friend. Well, she's sexy, experimental, and lots of fun, as you can see. She chose all the clothes, and I chose the situations. This photo shoot lasted until 2 A.M.

136 DAVID BALL

Shot in Colorado, at night.

137 BROOKS AND DUNN

I shot Kix and Ronnie separately, and then assembled this picture in the darkroom.

138/139 CONFEDERATE RAILROAD

This shot was a quicky. It was 6 A.M. The guys hopped out of their bus. We shot a few frames. It started to rain. They hopped back on the bus. That was it.

140 NANCI GRIFFITH

Nashville songwriter par excellence, I attended the premiere of "This Heart," which she wrote and performed with the Nashville ballet (no, she didn't dance; she played the guitar). Recently she also recorded and performed with Buddy Holly's original band, The Crickets, seen on the opposite page—which was the inspiration for this guitar-slingin' shot. Nanci has a unique voice and a style all her own.

141 THE CRICKETS

As kids, they were a hot rock and roll sensation, with their pal, Buddy Holly. As adults, they live deep in the Tennessee countryside, as farmers. But still performing as a band, they can really rock out. In this photo, JR, in the center, is wearing a cap that actually belonged to Buddy Holly.

142/143 BLACKHAWK

Photographed backstage at Farm Aid, the 1995 edition, where they appeared as the special guests of Willie Nelson.

144/145 GEORGE JONES AND TAMMY WYNETTE

Although George and Tammy are divorced, and both have since remarried, they are certainly the single most legendary couple in country music. Stories of George's drinking days and wild antics are endless; Tammy sported the original "big ha'ar" do. After years of not even speaking, Tammy and George finally went on the road together for the first and who knows, maybe the last time. I attended a concert where so many adoring fans were throwing themselves at the stage, I had to get out of the way to avoid getting crushed.

146/147 LeANN RIMES

Teen singer LeAnn Rimes reminds me of Tanya Tucker at the same age—same sexy quality, same confidence, same little girl/big girl dichotomy, same blonde hair. And, like Tanya, she is managed by her father. I photographed her during "downtime" at a Crook and Chase TV show taping, in the hallway and in the makeup room. At a certain point she went off by herself to sing scales to warm up her vocal chords. Pretty impressive, I thought.

148/149 REBA McENTIRE

Although Reba is an artist, and head of a growing entertainment business entity called "Starstruck," which is housed in the newest and most expensive building on Music Row, I always seem to focus on her softer side. That's why I like these pictures.

150/151 GEORGE STRAIT

George Strait is a country-singing superstar and a rancher. I've been told he has a mega-spread, 15,000 acres in south Texas, where he spends most of his time. Here he's pictured with his new puppy (named Ben), an Australian Cattle Dog, a gift from his record company.

152/153 JUNIOR BROWN

Junior records the most unusual songs in country music, singing in a very deep, kind of monotonal bass voice. He's unusual looking also, for any musical genre, and he plays a unique musical instrument, the guit-steel, a combination guitar and steel guitar. Here he projects his retro-but-real image for the camera.

158/159 OAK RIDGE BOYS

This photo was taken late in the afternoon on the grounds of Rock Castle in Hendersonville, Tennessee. Like the oak trees behind them, the golden light makes the group appear monumental. It seemed extremely ironic that shortly after this picture was taken Steve Sanders, (second from the left), abruptly resigned from the group.

161 MARK COLLIE

Mark lives in beautiful Williamson County, Tennessee, about 30 miles outside of Nashville. With its rolling hills and green pastures, its easy to see why so many stars live there. Mark and I just went for a ride in the country; and when we saw this endless row of hay bales, we went for it.

164/165 PERFECT STRANGER

Out of East Texas, Perfect Stranger created their own answer to the question of how to break into the country music business. They spent their own money to produce their first record and first video, and burned up three vans before they could finally afford a bus. Ironically, their first single was well on its way to being #1 when they finally signed a record deal.

154/155/156/157 SHELBY LYNNE

This photo shoot was the greatest! Shelby is great at everything she does, whether its singing, writing, performing, or having her picture taken. A true chameleon, since this session she's changed her hair color to white blonde—I guess we'll just have to do these pictures again. During our photo session, we got along so well, we stopped talking entirely and communed instead of communicating.

160 WILLIAM GOLDEN

After a short search for a replacement, William Golden was recruited to rejoin the Oak Ridge Boys. It was readily apparent that his deep bass voice contributes a very special quality to the Oaks sound. As a friend of mine put it, "I didn't miss him until he came back."

162/163 SWEETHEARTS OF THE RODEO

Janis Gill (wife of country star Vince Gill) and her sister Kristine Arnold are the Sweethearts. In addition to their recording career (they have been nominated by the CMA as Vocal Duo of the Year for ten straight years), they own several very fashionable women's apparel shops called Gill and Arnold. This picture was taken after the Franklin Rotary Club Rodeo parade, for which they were the Grand Marshals.

166 DAVID LEE MURPHY

When I asked David Lee's manager to describe him, he said "redneck," but he meant it in the nicest way. Even though he has several #1 hits behind him and unique good looks, he still lives deep in the country.

167/168/169 THE MAVERICKS

Originally from Miami, the Mavericks are unique to country music. A fun-loving group of guys, these pictures were taken just before they headed off to win a CMA Award.

170/171 THE HIGHWAYMEN

Do these faces look familiar? They should, because they belong to four legendary country music stars. Johnny Cash, Willie Nelson, Kris Kristofferson, and Waylon Jennings make up the band. As they say, "The road goes on forever and the party never ends."

172/173 PATTY LOVELESS

I found this old tintype photo book at a flea market in Leipers Fork. I removed the original pictures of Aunt Anna and Great Grandpa and put in these fun ones of Patty Loveless.

174/175 STEVE EARLE

I got the idea to put Steve on this tricycle the day before the shoot. It came from the name of his record, "Train's A Comin'," and from the fact that there were some neat train tracks right near my photo studio. Steve was worried that the police would come and arrest him, since he's still on parole, while I kept hoping that a train would come (in the background).

176/177 NASHVILLE SONGWRITERS ASSOCIATION INTERNATIONAL

Because the song is that from which all else springs in the country music business, I didn't want to forget to tip my (photographic) hat to some of the legends in the business, the NSAI board. They are (top) Dennis Lord, Kenny O'Dell, Pat Alger, Angela Kaset, James Dean Hicks, Bob DiPiero, Thom Schuyler, Sandy Knox, Executive Director Carol Fox, Randy Goodrum, Jim McBride, Cinda Hargrove, and Lisa Palas; (bottom) Allen Shamblin, Carol Etheridge, Jon Vezner, Wayland Holyfield, Layng Martine, Jr.

178 DAVIS DANIEL

Because I think Davis is one of the hunkiest of the new country singers, I wanted to portray him that way.

179 JOHN BERRY John Berry sings like an angel and rides a big Harley motorcycle. His wife is a backup singer in his band, and he travels with his children.

180/181 SAMMY KERSHAW Sammy wanted only one thing from this photo session: he wanted to be shot smoking!

182/183 WADE HAYES I first saw Wade backstage at the Ryman immediately after he opened a show for Merle Haggard. Since it was his first-ever Ryman appearance, he was pretty happy. Even with the "hat hair," I thought he looked pretty good. Months later, I photographed him again in the studio to show another side of Wade.

184 MARY CHAPIN CARPENTER This is one of the very few performance shots in this book.

185 ALISON KRAUSS Alison Krauss is the youngest member of the Grand Ole Opry, and a very independent individual. I heard her interviewed on the radio one morning from a hotel room somewhere (I gathered she was sleeping when the jock called her room). She definitely arose to the occasion, and was very funny. Nonetheless, it reminded me once again of how hard it is to be an artist on the road.

186 TRACY BYRD I photographed Tracy's CD cover *Big Love* in the Rocky Mountains. This photo was taken during a break from his video shoot.

187 I took this picture when I first met Tracy, several months before doing his CD cover. I thought it was a fitting image to end this book. Goodnight, y'all!

autographs

autographs

about the photographer

Raeanne Rubenstein was born on Staten Island, New York. She attended the University of Pennsylvania, in Philadelphia, where she studied English literature, and graduated with honors. While there, she studied photography at the Annenberg school and took pictures as a hobby.

After college, she moved to London, where she apprenticed with a well-known fashion photographer, before moving back to New York. In New York, she assisted by day, and photographed rock concerts, theatrical performances, poetry readings, and other events at night. After some time, she began to get assignments to shoot these events, and quit her day job.

As time passed she got more assignments, working for many magazines, record companies, movie companies, book publishers, advertising agencies and TV networks, shooting celebrities. In 1975, she produced *Honkytonk Heroes*, her first photo book of country music stars.

In addition, her work can be seen in various galleries and museum collections. A nationwide tour of photographs from *Gone Country* will begin at the Country Music Hall of Fame in Nashville this summer.

She has won many design awards, including a recent one for a series of computer-manipulated celebrity portraits.